I0422593

A Massachusetts Conservative in the Cradle of Liberty

A Massachusetts Conservative in the Cradle of Liberty

My Run for Congress in
Massachusetts—2004

Chuck Morse

iUniverse, Inc.
New York Lincoln Shanghai

A Massachusetts Conservative in the Cradle of Liberty
My Run for Congress in Massachusetts—2004

All Rights Reserved © 2004 by Charles A. Morse

No part of this book may be reproduced or transmitted in any form or by any means, graphic, electronic, or mechanical, including photocopying, recording, taping, or by any information storage retrieval system, without the written permission of the publisher.

iUniverse, Inc.

For information address:
iUniverse, Inc.
2021 Pine Lake Road, Suite 100
Lincoln, NE 68512
www.iuniverse.com

ISBN: 0-595-33855-0

Printed in the United States of America

With great appreciation to those who helped my campaign for Congress

Rev. Rick Barr, Martin Begian, Sam Blumenfeld, Anthony Ciciariello, Brock Cordiero, Janet Dow, Jody Dow, Ambassador Ray Flynn, Peter and Sylvia Friedman, Peter Gadiel, Albert Garrison, Gloria Gavris, Ed Guy, former U.S. Representative Margaret Heckler, Arthur Larrivee, Ralph Medeiros, Chris McCarthy, Jim Neihuis, Phil Paleologos, Carl and Donna Pasquarosa, Pete Peterson, David and Donna Raposa, Michael Robbins, Matt Santos, Ralph Saulnier, Ben Shapiro, Frank Shaw, Parky Shaw, Michael and Barbara Stedman, and Rob Sudduph.

Special and profound thanks to my wife, Barbara Morse, and to my chief campaign advisor Ben Kilgore

Contents

Entering the Race

I decided to run for Congress in 2004 after analyzing the race and becoming convinced that it was winnable. I couldn't resist the opportunity to offer the voters of the 4th congressional district of Massachusetts a genuine choice between Barney Frank, the ultra-liberal 12-term incumbent and myself, a conservative small business owner, taxpayer, property owner, husband, father, radio talk show host, and author. There had not been a real race in the district since Frank beat the Republican incumbent congresswomen, Margaret M. Heckler, in 1981. Since that time, Frank has had little or no opposition. Yet, I believed that the district was changing and my hope was that I could catch the wave of that change.

When I arrived at my decision to run, Massachusetts no longer appeared to be the liberal bastion that the rest of the country perceived us to be. The bloom had been knocked off the liberal rose back in 1988 with the defeat of Michael Dukakis as the Democratic Presidential nominee. Dukakis, while carrying his home state, didn't do as well as expected in his run against George Bush Sr. Massachusetts residents knew that the Dukakis campaign boast to the nation of presiding over a "Massachusetts miracle" was a gross exaggeration. The size of the state government had ballooned in the 1980's, crime was up, unemployment and welfare dependency were at an all time high and taxes were among the highest in the nation during his tenure. Dukakis last two lame duck years in office after his presidential defeat were a disheartening and pathetic spectacle.

The election of Republican U.S. Attorney William F. Weld as Governor of Massachusetts in 1990 represented the first step toward a more conservative government. Weld was a fiscal conservative who held the line on taxes and began the laborious process of streamlining the colossal and patronage laden state system. In his first year in office, Weld proved Dukakis wrong in his dire prediction that people would be starving in the streets unless an immediate tax increase was passed by the legislature. As Weld began hosing down the Augean stables of Massachusetts state government, Massachusetts began to experience a newfound sense of vibrancy.

Venture capitalist Mitt Romney, who had run a vigorous and stylish campaign in 1994 against liberal icon Senator Ted Kennedy, continued the conservative Massachusetts revolution with an impressive victory in his race for Governor over Democratic State Treasurer Shannon O'Brien in 2002. O'Brien was a throwback to the bad old days of liberal hack-infested bureaucracies with friends and relatives on payrolls and a culture of government largess. Besides running on a platform of fiscal reform and holding the line on taxes, Mitt Romney was more conservative on social issues than his more socially liberal Republican predecessors, Governors Bill Weld, Paul Cellucci and Jane Swift.

By 2003, when I made my decision to run, the 4th congressional district and the state in general seemed to be continuing in a trend toward conservatism. Mitt Romney had almost won in the liberal 4th congressional district and had carried 65% of its cities and towns. O'Brien had only won by a nose in a district known to be a liberal sinecure for Barney Frank. O'Brien barely eked out a victory even though a big Democratic rally was held for her on election eve in downtown New Bedford and Democratic heavy guns such as Ted Kennedy and former President Bill Clinton were trotted out.

Along with the election of Mitt Romney, a proposition on the ballot that year, sponsored by Citizens for Limited Taxation and Government, would have abolished the state income tax entirely. It garnered 47% of the vote in spite of opposition from both major party candidates. The election had taken the temperature of the voters and the message sent was "no more taxes."

The fourth congressional district snakes from suburban Boston to the south coast of Massachusetts like a python. At its head are the liberal Boston bedroom communities of Brookline and Newton. The district then continues west into Wellesley, traditionally a conservative stronghold that has trended liberal in recent years and the Republican strongholds of Dover and Sherborn. Heading south, the district includes the relatively conservative middle class towns of Millis, Norfolk, Foxborough, Mansfield and Norton with the more liberal Sharon cobbled on.

Heading further south, the district includes most of southeastern Massachusetts including the entire south coast region stretching from Wareham, a summer beach community bordering Cape Cod, to Westport, home of Horseneck Beach, one of the finest beaches in New England. At the center of the south coast, both literally and spiritually, sits the great and historic whaling and manufacturing port of New Bedford. Near Rhode Island, the district includes half of Spindle City, the great old textile city of Fall River, and all of Silver City, the historic manufacturing city of Taunton. Other cities and towns include Middleboro, known for cranberry bogs and small manufacturing, and the towns of Halifax, Lakeville, Freetown, Rochester, Berkeley, Raynham, Dighton, Fairhaven, Acushnet and the fashionable coastal towns of Marion, Mattapoisett, and Dartmouth.

The communities of south coast surrounding New Bedford, Fall River, and Taunton are growing in population and changing with young families buying and building new and beautiful homes. This is a region where a family starting out can still purchase land and build a house at a relatively low cost, compared to other parts of the state. The forests, swamps, lakes, beaches and coastline are among the most beautiful and pristine in the northeastern United States. Cranberry growing remains a major industry in the region and the port of New Bedford-Fairhaven is the largest fishing port in the North Atlantic.

Old-fashioned Democratic political machines control New Bedford, Fall River, and Taunton. These cities never fully rebounded from the flight of manufacturing industries, which accelerated back in the 1950's with the closing of Hathaway Mills in New Bedford. Instead of catching the wave of the new high tech industry and small business, these cities, particularly New Bedford and Fall River, have tended to stagnate with high unemployment rates and have built massive public housing projects encouraged by ill-conceived federal housing grants. As is the case whenever there are large concentrations of unemployed men, these cities have seen an increase in crime, drugs, and murder.

I didn't expect my candidacy to break the stranglehold the Democrats had on these cities, with their support of poverty programs and public housing, but I did hope to offer an alternative to the status quo. I believed that if I could get my message out, I could contribute in some way toward changing the culture in the region. My message was pro business, pro private ownership, and strongly supportive of Governor Romney's efforts to reform state government.

I argued that my opponent was a part of the problem, given his sub par record regarding business. He had a zero rating with non-partisan groups who rate Congressmen in terms of how they vote on business interests. Those groups included the National Federation of Independent Businessmen (NFIB), and the American Association of Builders and Contractors (AABC). Frank also had a low rating with the U.S. Chamber of Commerce. When I brought this aspect of my opponent's voting record up during our debates, he responded by referring to these groups as "right-wing" and "very right-wing." If being pro business is right wing, then I wear the moniker proudly. The best social program is, after all, a job.

My opponent had a zero rating with the American Taxpayers Union. This non-partisan group, which rates Congressmen on their voting record with regard to support of low taxes and spending, has as its Massachusetts affiliate Barbara Anderson's Citizens for a Limited Taxation and Government. I support their work on behalf of taxpayers. I also support the tax cuts of President George W. Bush, which my opponent voted against.

The Boston Globe acknowledged that the Bush tax cuts helped the economy turn the corner on the recession. At the time I announced my candidacy, the economy was improving and jobs were increasing. I made the case that my opponent's votes against tax cuts, including a vote against making the Bush $1,000 child tax credit permanent, were regressive and hurtful to working people. After all, I reasoned, this wasn't a tax cut for the rich. $1,000 is a lot of money for a working family with children.

Barney Frank just doesn't understand the entrepreneurial spirit. He has never used the considerable influence that comes with being a Congressman to try to persuade businesses to locate in the district. Besides voting against legislation that would've made doing business easier, and voting for high taxes, my opponent had done nothing in terms of getting federal funding for the critically needed New Bedford—Fall River commuter rail.

An example of this lack of interest was my opponent's response to the Sovereign Bank buyout of the New Bedford based Compass Bank, which occurred in July 2004. The buyout resulted in the shutting down of Compass Bank, which had been in business in New Bedford in some form or another since the 19th century. This resulted in the layoff of 350 employees and the closing down of an architecturally significant office building in downtown New Bedford.

My opponent had grabbed headlines in the New Bedford Standard-Times in February of that year, when talk of the buyout had become public, demanding that Sovereign honor commitments made to New Bedford by Compass under the community reinvestment act and that the bank not lay people off. The Standard-Times published a full-page open letter sent by my opponent to the CEO of Sovereign making these demands. Five months later, while Barney Frank was being wined and dined at an award ceremony held in his honor at the exclusive Bay Tower Club by the influential Financial Services Roundtable, the merger took place and the pink slips went out in New Bedford.

The Bay Tower gala honoring Frank occurred during the Democratic National Convention held in Boston. Massachusetts Senator John Kerry was nominated for President. Barney Frank took the opportunity to let it be known that in the event Kerry won the Presidency, he would seek the Senate seat vacated by Kerry. Around this time, Frank began receiving hundreds of thousands of dollars in donations from banking interests. Frank was the ranking Democrat on the Congressional Financial Services Committee, which oversees banking legislation. Fred Wertheimer, head of the liberal watchdog group Democracy 21, referred to Frank's activities as inappropriate and as a possible conflict of interest in an interview he granted to the Boston Globe.

Barney Frank is the beneficiary of one of the most gerrymandered districts in the country, which is why he gets away with repeated abuses of his position. Boston Globe columnist Joan Vennochi, in a June 17th column "Strong-arm tactics could backfire on Mass. Democrats" delved into the history of the district when she interviewed former 4th congressional district Republican Congresswomen Margaret M. Heckler, who discussed how U.S. House Speaker Thomas P. "Tip" O'Neill had personally crafted the district in 1981 to ensure she would lose her re-election bid. Prompted by the redistricting, O'Neill's anointed protégé, Massachusetts State Rep. Barney Frank, who represented the Back Bay neighborhood of Boston at the time, would quickly move into the district and run for the seat.

Heckler told Vennochi that the stage was set for a showdown between her and Tip O'Neill after she voted in favor of President Ronald Reagan's budget and tax cutting proposal in 1981. Heckler recalled that when she told Reagan that she was supporting his budget, Vice President George Bush, in the room during the conversation, said, "She is going to pay the price." Heckler said that the vote "cost me the election…Tip O'Neill was shocked…he was furious at me. I knew it in my bones. I knew it was a sacrificial vote."

When I entered the race, I expected and looked forward to a vigorous and tough contest against one of the most powerful and pampered members of Congress. I would not shy away from bringing up tough issues and had already done so from the beginning when I pointed out, upon entering the race, that Frank's no vote on the Amber Alert bill, which protects children from kidnappers, was the issue that finally caused me to decide to run. I was running for Congress as a concerned father.

Naturally, Frank struck back hard. In a contest where two opposing ideologies are at play, there ought to be a fierce fight. We were fighting for the hearts and souls of the voters of the district. My candidacy offered the voters an opportunity to change the political and ideological fault lines of the state.

The American election represents an opportunity for the citizenry to effect a peaceful and orderly revolution and the results reflect the direction in which the country is going. With profound issues at stake, issues that will affect our futures on many different levels, it should be expected that the contest would be rigorous. Those who want nice orderly elections where everyone smiles and gets along might consider moving to Cuba, where elections are always tidy.

Aiding & Abetting

One of the secrets of Barney Frank's longevity as a Congressman is his wit; he is funny and quick with the ironic riposte. Another is the fact that no reporter has delved too deeply into his 24-year record in Congress. If such an examination were to be reported on, especially in the area of immigration, not only would Barney Frank have been long gone and forgotten, but the voters of the district would've long ago sent his into retirement.

Frank is protected and coddled by friends in the liberal establishment and the media. As a result, he has been able to freely dabble into legislative waters that other congressman, fearful of opposition and not enjoying such protection, would fear to tread. Every piece of legislation he has filed, starting in 1981, is available to the public online at Thomas, which is the official congressional archival website. I doubt the media has ever consulted these archives and they make for some pretty eye opening reading.

I was first made aware of the Frank amendment, one of a long list of amendments to the Immigration and Nationality Act the Congressman has sponsored almost every session, when a supporter emailed me excerpts from "Why America Slept—The Failure to Prevent 9/11" by Gerald Posner. Posner, a former Wall Street lawyer, award-winning author of eight books, frequent guest commentator on TV, writer for the New York Times, The New Yorker, Newsweek, the Wall Street Journal and U.S.News and World Report, with a reputation as a liberal investigative journalist, had written this expose to document events that led up to the terrorist attack on the World Trade Center and the Pentagon. This was no right-wing book, but rather a New York Times bestseller soon to be made into a Showtime miniseries, published by Ballantine Books, a subsidiary of Simon and Schuster.

Barney Frank is specifically mentioned in this book. "Why America Slept," which has been just released in paperback and is available in all major bookstores across the country, offers the following excerpt (page 17–18):

"Ronald Reagan might have named the Soviet Union as his primary foreign policy nemesis, but Islamic extremists were getting his attention and increasingly making the United States look vulnerable and weak. From the 1983 bombing of the marine barracks in Lebanon that killed 241 soldiers to the 1985 hijackings of TWA flight 847 and the cruise liner Achille Lauro, Middle Eastern terror was now on the White House's priority agenda.

"Senior CIA officers complained to the president's national security team about their frustration with the FBI and warned that America was vulnerable to Islamic terrorists entering on legal visas and setting up sleeper cells.

"Reagan responded in September 1986 by forming an interagency task force, the Alien Border Control Committee (ABCC), whose purpose was to block entry of suspected terrorists and to deport militants who either had come into the country illegally or had overstayed their visas. The CIA and FBI joined the ABCC effort.

"Six months after its formation, the ABCC had its first notable success. The CIA tipped off the FBI to a group of suspected Palestinian terrorists in Los Angeles. The Bureau arrested eight men. But instead of being lauded, the Bureau and the Agency came under harsh attack from civil liberties groups who argued that the ABCC should be banned from using any information the CIA gained from the government's routine processing of visa requests.

"Congressman Barney Frank, the Massachusetts Democrat who was a strong advocate of protecting civil liberties, led a successful effort to amend the Immigration and Nationality Act so that membership in a terrorist group was no longer sufficient to deny a visa.

"Under Frank's amendment, which seems unthinkable post 9/11, a visa could only be denied if the government could prove that the applicant had committed an act of terrorism. Rendered toothless by the Frank amendment, the Reagan Administration had virtually no way to block entry visas even when there was information linking the individuals to terrorist groups."

According to Posner, the Frank amendment undid an earnest attempt by the Reagan Administration in the 1980's to coordinate and integrate security and intelligence gathering agencies under the umbrella of the ABCC. This lack of coordination and cohesiveness on the part of our security agencies was very much responsible for a breakdown in our government's ability to effectively protect us from terrorism. The 9/11 terrorists detected this state of paralysis, according to the 9/11-commission report. Terrorists and those who aided and abetted their activities were able to operate with a relatively free hand in the years between 1989, when the Frank amendment went into effect, in preparation for the attack on September 11th 2001.

Reagan's ABCC, rendered toothless by the Frank amendment according to Posner, would be resurrected decades later with the USA Patriot Act and the creation of the Department of Homeland Security. This would unfortunately occur only after the devastation of 9/11, the infiltration of untold numbers of terrorists into this country and the possible setting up of unknown numbers of terrorist sleeper cells. Ironically, Barney Frank, the chief sponsor of the law that greatly contributed to this situation, is now a member of the Congressional committee on homeland security. This is a travesty given the damage caused by his amendment and other legislation he has consistently sponsored over his 24-year career in Congress. During the campaign, I called upon the Congressman to resign from that committee and that challenge still stands.

I attended a luncheon in Washington D.C. during the campaign at which Secretary of Homeland Security Tom Ridge was the keynote speaker. Secretary Ridge noted that not a single day goes by without the department he heads receiving credible tips concerning threats by terrorist sleeper cells and other sources. It will no doubt take many years, even decades, to undo the terrible damage done to this country by the Frank amendment and other misguided policies.

Congressman Frank stated during our debates that his motivation in crafting the Frank amendment was his contention that it was inappropriate for our government to deny visas to people such as the communist novelist Gabriel Garcia Marquez, a close associate of the Cuban dictator Fidel Castro. Frank described Marquez in an article as "a distinguished literary and political figure." He claimed that his legislation served the purpose of undoing outdated Cold War laws that excluded members and affiliates of the Communist Party. In an essay, Frank signed and posted on his congressional website, October 10, 2001, four weeks after 9/11, entitled "Barney Frank's Views on the Terrorism Bill" Frank complained "America was frequently embarrassed" by the "exclusion of foreigners whose political views various Americans found objectionable."

Putting aside the snide swipe at those of us who might object to a friend of the bloody tyrant Castro visiting this country to make satchels full of money selling books to elitist college students attending ivy league colleges, a fraud like Marquez would only pose as a threat to the trust funds of those inclined to consider his ilk to be a "distinguished literary and political figure."

The fact of the matter is that such a figure as Marquez could've most likely been cleared to enter without the Frank amendment. To the extent that legislation might have been called for to help the likes of Marques find clearance, and to undo specific aspects of the Cold War laws in question, appropriate legislation could've been crafted to deal with specific cases. Frank's heavy handed and sweeping legislation instead made it easier for everyone with a political agenda to come into the country on a visa.

The problem with the Frank amendment is that it effectively hamstrung the government's ability to deny visas to anyone based upon their political orientation. This would come to include people affiliated with such groups as Hamas and the 19 hijackers who turned passenger planes into missiles on September 11th and used those planes to kill 3,000 people. None of the Hamas affiliates or hijackers who entered this country legally thanks to the Frank amendment were formally affiliated with a group deemed by the State Department as involved in terrorism, nor were they involved in "terrorist activities" by the classic definition of the term.

The net effect of the Frank amendment was that it became more difficult for the government to prove a connection between the visa applicant and the terrorist activities. It should be noted that Frank fought for this legislation, which he considered in his fecund imagination to be progressive, at a time when the terrorist threat was well known. Terrorists already demonstrated their ability to ruthlessly kill American citizens. It is unprecedented in international law and custom for any sovereign state, today or in history, to be made vulnerable in such a manner.

In this same signed essay, the Congressman defended his amendment with the incredulous rationalization that since American citizens have the right to free speech and free expression, those rights ought to be extended to foreigners who want to come here to express themselves. He argues that our right to free expression is somehow "impinged when we exclude people because we find their political views unpopular, unsettling, or dangerous." In other words, the Congressman believes that our right to free speech and expression is denied if our government doesn't let a foreigner come into the country to expose us to his speech and expression. This inexplicable premise constitutes, essentially, an extension of first amendment rights, guaranteed by the American Constitution to American citizens residing in America, to virtually anyone in the world.

The Congressman goes on to write that the mere "espousal or endorsement of terrorist activity casts too wide a net of exclusion." Really? This is why Sami al-Arian was able to get a visa to teach at the University of Florida while raising money for Islamic "charities" that would then funnel the money to Hamas. It would've been difficult for the government to prove that al-Arian was associated with Hamas even though he was caught on video delivering a speech in Chicago where he clearly was engaging in the "espousal or endorsement of terrorist activity." Had it not been for the Frank amendment, and had President Reagan's ABCC been allowed to do its job, Sami al-Arian, a non-citizen, would've probably been detained and deported.

Frank thinks that decisions made by immigration officials regarding the denial of visas ought to undergo judicial review. This aspect of the legislation filed by the Congressman, requiring that both immigration officials and foreign ambassadors submit a denial of a visa to judicial review, has made it more difficult for our elected officials and their appointed representatives to deny visas. The Constitution does not grant the judicial branch of government the power to review visa applications. In fact, the setting of immigration policy has traditionally resided solely with the executive. The President traditionally retained the power to set visa policy under the same principle that gives the President the power to set foreign or diplomatic policy. This effectively set up another hoop immigration officials and ambassadors would have to jump through before denying a visa to someone who, in their judgment, should not be let in.

Frank complains in the article that without judicial review, immigration officials, acting according to directives from the executive, might be able to exclude "supporters of the African National Congress or the Irish Republican Army." But why shouldn't our elected leaders decide whether any member of any group, for whatever reason, should be granted the right to visit this country?

Visiting this country is not a right but a privilege, and the setting of guidelines regarding who should be allowed to visit ought to reside with officials elected to represent the interests and aspirations of those who elect them. This is the constitutional and democratic approach.

President John Adams codified this principle into law when he signed the Aliens Enemies Act in 1798, a law that protected this country for almost two hundred years. This law, a version of which is in place within the laws of every sovereign nation in existence today or in history, expresses one of the most basic functions of national sovereignty. As individuals, we decide who is invited into our homes. There are laws that protect this right. Nations have the same natural right. Indeed nations are charged with a practical and a moral responsibility to exercise that same right in order to protect the national home. Any attempt to try to subvert those rights is a formula for catastrophe, as we have seen.

Frank does not think the government should have the right to deny visas to those deemed to be terrorists for political reasons. In other words, to Frank's way of thinking, it isn't enough for a person to espouse terrorism; a person would have to be proven to have engaged in terrorist activity to be denied a visa. To make his argument, he complains in the article that Nelson Mandela and Gerry Adams were excluded from entering the country because they were declared to be terrorists by the government.

He points out that the Clinton Administration was able to exclude Adams even after the passage of his amendment as proof that the government was still able to deny entry even with his amendment in place, but this entirely misses the point. In a specific case, the President or the Attorney General could override the Frank amendment and deny a visa to a specific person, but what about the thousands of everyday applicants who might be entering in order to form sleeper cells? Gerry Adams was the exception to the rule and, by the way, many people in Boston might remember cases of arms smuggling for the Irish Republican Army emanating out of Boston in the 1970's. The Frank amendment created a roadblock for our immigration officials and ambassadors.

Frank states in the article that he was concerned that the "endorsed or espoused" part of his amendment, if removed by the USA Patriot Act, "could lead to a renewal of some restriction on people whom Americans should continue to have a right to hear if they so choose." Since when does the right of Americans to hear whatever they choose to hear mean that the expositors of views deemed to be detrimental to the country have a right to come here and to express those views? Using this twisted logic, hatemongering neo-Nazis or ideological support-ers of Osama bin Laden, not formally connected to "terrorist activities," would have the right to visit the country, get their followers to rent out halls and pro-mote their appearances, and then give speeches spewing hatred and racism. Unfortunately, this is exactly what happened after the Frank amendment became law.

No such right has ever been granted by this or any nation to foreigners until Frank came along. According to award winning researcher and documentary filmmaker Steven Emerson, this type of activity started in earnest in the 1990's. This was after the Frank amendment went into effect. For example, according to Emerson, followers of the ideology of Hamas started visiting the country on Frank amendment visas to deliver hate filled speeches to jam-packed Mosques and halls. These events were used to scout out and recruit potential terrorists. Our INS and overseas embassies were turned into revolving turnstiles for those advocating views that were "unpopular, unsettling, or dangerous." A nation must at all times, as a basic article of survival, retain the right to exclude those who seek to enter for the purpose of espousing and fomenting religious intolerance and ethnic hatred.

Barney Frank's inept meddling into immigration policy over his long career in Congress was the central and defining issue of the race. The core question which I raised was whether the nineteen 9/11 hijackers had arrived in this country legally and, if so, to what degree did the Frank amendment play a facilitating role. Several times during our debates and on Newsnight with Chet Curtis and Jim Braude on NECN, Frank, in response to my accusation, stated flatly that the hijackers were here illegally. That assertion was misleading. The hijackers may have technically been here illegally at the exact time of the hijacking but this was only because their legally obtained student and travel visas had expired. Had Reagan's ABCC been left in place to do its job back in 1985, the hijackers would probably never have gotten into the country, or if they did, they would've most likely been detained and expelled.

Regarding the terrorist hijackers, the "9–11 Commission Report" states (p. 237):

The muscle hijackers began arriving in the United States in late April 2001. In most cases they traveled in pairs on tourist visas and entered the United States in Orlando or Miami, Florida; Washington D.C.; or New York. Atta and Shehhi assisted those arriving in Florida, while Hazmi and Hanjour took care of the rest. By the end of June, 14 of the 15 muscle hijackers had crossed the Atlantic.

The September 11th terrorist ringleaders included:

Mohamed Atta, leader of the hijackers, who landed in Newark, N.J., from Prague on a visitor's visa issued in Berlin on June 3, 1999. He crashed American Airlines Flight 11 into the South Tower of the World Trade Center;

Ziad al-Jarrah, the pilot of United Airlines Flight 93, which crashed in Pennsylvania. He received his pilot's license in Hamburg, Germany, and entered the United States on June 27 at Newark;

Marwan al Shehhi, pilot of United Airlines Flight 175, which crashed into the North Tower. He arrived in the United States at Newark on May 29, 2000, on a tourist visa issued in the United Arab Emirates, and cleared customs in less than a half-hour;

Hani Honjour, pilot of American Airlines Flight 77, which crashed into the Pentagon. He first entered the United States on a student visa in 1996, returned to Saudi Arabia, then traveled from the United Arab Emirates back to the United States in December 2000 on a student visa.

Relevant amendments to the Immigration and Nationality Act sponsored by Barney Frank include:

1. ***H.R. 5287*** Introduced 12/16/1981
Title: *A bill to amend the Immigration and Nationality Act with respect to aliens who seek to enter the United States to do research at colleges and universities…within the definition of "aliens who are members of the teaching profession or who have exceptional ability in the sciences or the arts."*

This was part of a trend toward liberalizing the issuance of student visas. While it is appropriate for foreign students from friendly countries to obtain visas to attend college, this bill makes no provision for the monitoring of those students to insure that they are in school. A law of this nature makes it easier for, say, a "student" from North Korea to study nuclear physics at M.I.T., or a Palestinian "student" to study explosives. Several of the 9/11 hijackers were holders of student visas. Flight 77 hijacker Hani Hanjour held a student visa while never attending a school. Both hijackers Mohammed Atta and Marwan al-Shehi arranged to have their tourist visas changed to student visas because they knew that laws governing student visas were more liberal.

2. *H.R. 4509* Introduced 11/18/1983
Title: *A bill to amend the Immigration and Nationality Act with respect to the grounds for exclusion and deportation of aliens.*

This bill codifies into law several categories for exclusion that already existed in the law before the bill was crafted. The bill makes the following changes to the already existing law regarding which applicants for visas would be excludable:

(4) any alien convicted of two or more offenses for which the aggregate sentences actually imposed were five years or more.

This would lower the bar with regard to visas for convicted criminals. This means that if the applicant had spent less than 5 years in prison, or was convicted of only one crime, than a visa could not be denied.

(7) any alien deemed by the Attorney General as a probable security risk for certain specified reasons.

This would raise the bar in terms of what constituted a security risk. The Attorney General would have less discretion under this law as evidence would now have to be presented that would have to involve specified reasons for denying a visa as opposed to judgment, suspicion or second hand information. Under this rule, it would be more difficult to prove that the applicant was a security risk.

(8) any alien who is an active member of an organization engaged in violence or terrorist activities.

What about inactive membership? What about indirect support or expressed sympathies? During the cold war years, the communists used to get around this by simply having their operatives not join the party. Certainly al Quada is not an organization in the formal sense with membership.

Makes deportable by the Attorney General only those aliens within one of the following classes: (9) any alien who at any time is convicted on any of various specified loyalty laws (e.g. sabotage, treason and sedition, selective service, etc..) (12) any alien engaging in activity which endangers the public safety or national security;

None of the 9/11 hijackers, none of the Hamas members operating in this country in the 1990's, were actively involved in sabotage. Treasonous and seditious activities are extremely difficult to prove. The hijackers and the Hamas members operated entirely, in fact quite scrupulously, within the color of the law while they engaged in their activities. They didn't engage in activities that could easily be discerned as endangering public safety or national security. Hamas sent money overseas to fund those activities in other countries and the 9/11 hijackers planned and waited until 9/11 before violating "various specified loyalty laws."

3. ***H.R. 5227*** Introduced 3/22/1984
Title: *A bill to amend the Immigration and Nationality Act with respect to the grounds for exclusion and deportation of aliens.*

This act is virtually identical to H.R. 4509, filed 4 months previous except for the following provision:

Repeals provisions dealing with bond and conditions for admission for permanent residence for retarded, tubercular, and mentally ill aliens.

4. ***H.R.2361*** Introduced 5/6/1985
Title: *A bill to amend the Immigration and Nationality Act with respect to the grounds for exclusion and deportation of aliens.*

This act is virtually identical with the one filed in 1984 except for the following relevant changes:

(6) any alien who has engaged in terrorist activity against the United States or against a citizen of the United States.

(8) any alien deemed by the Attorney General as a probable security risk for certain specified reasons, including terrorist activity.

(14) any alien who has engaged in terrorist activity against the United States or against a citizen of the United States.

5. H.R.1119 Introduced 2/18/1987
Title: *A bill to amend the Immigration and Nationality Act with respect to the grounds for exclusion and deportation of aliens.*

6. H.R. 4427 Introduced 4/20/1988
Title: *A bill to amend the Immigration and Nationality Act with respect to the grounds for exclusion and deportation of aliens.*

This is the Frank Amendment. This is the law responsible for opening the floodgates to terrorists. This law contains the following sentence:

Repeals the ideological grounds for exclusion.

7. H.R.1280 Introduced 3/7/1989
Title: *To amend the Immigration and Nationality Act with respect to grounds for exclusion and deportation of aliens.*

Repeals the ideological grounds for exclusion.

8. **H.R.3305** Introduced 10/19/1993
Title: *To amend the Immigration and Nationality Act to establish a Board of Visa Appeals within the Department of State to review decisions of consular officers concerning visa applications, revocations and cancellations.*

This law would effectively create another hoop American Ambassadors would have to jump through before denying a visa to an applicant. The judgment of the Ambassador or indirect evidence of a connection to terrorism would not be enough to deny a visa under this law. Terrorist hijacker Mohammad Atta was granted a visitor's visa at the American Embassy in Berlin on June 3, 1999.

9. ***H.R.2975*** Introduced 2/27/1996
Title: *To amend the Immigration and Nationality Act to establish a Board of Visa Appeals within the Department of State to review decisions of consular officers concerning visa applications, revocations and cancellations.*

10. ***H.R.3928*** Introduced 7/31/1996
Title: *To amend the Immigration and Nationality Act with respect to waiver of exclusion for certain excludable aliens.*

11. ***H.R.4539*** Introduced 9/10/1998
Title: *To amend the Immigration and Nationality Act to establish a Board of Visa Appeals within the Department of State to review decisions of consular officers concerning visa applications, revocations and cancellations.*

12. ***H.R.1156*** Introduced 3/17/1999
Title: *To amend the Immigration and Nationality Act to establish a Board of Visa Appeals within the Department of State to review decisions of consular officers concerning visa applications, revocations, and cancellations.*

13. ***H.R. 1345*** Introduced 4/3/2001
Title: *To amend the Immigration and Nationality Act to establish a Board of Visa Appeals within the Department of State to review decisions of consular officers concerning visa applications, revocations, and cancellations.*

Issues 2004

The campaign focused on three general areas in the following order of importance, national security, the economy, and social issues. In the aftermath of the terrorist attack on September 11, 2001, no issue, in my opinion, was more important than the terrorist threat to this country and how our government was handling that threat. Issues such as economy, jobs, healthcare and abortion would be quickly rendered irrelevant if terrorists were, God forbid, able to seize a school and murder children or to detonate a dirty bomb in a downtown city.

National Security

America was, and remains, at risk of an attack from Islamic terrorists both from without and from within. One of my primary areas of historical research was the threat the Soviet Union and the international communist movement had posed to this country and the western democracies in the 20th century. I also authored a book on the origins of the modern Islamic terrorist movement called "The Nazi connection to Islamic Terrorism." The Islamic threat of today is in my opinion much more threatening and potentially more deadly than the communist movement ever was.

The United States and the Soviet Union were confined to co-exist within the narrow parameters of what was known as mutual assured destruction, otherwise known as MAD. This meant that both sides had their proverbial finger on the nuclear trigger and that any move by either side in an aggressive direction would be responded to with an equivalent counter move. The two nations stood on the dusty road at the OK corral looking into each other's eyes and waiting to see which side would blink. Neither side wanted to die on the road if the trigger was pulled and the world was blown to smithereens.

The Islamic terrorists know of no such constraints. Their radical interpretation of their faith, differing from the more moderate and peaceful Muslim interpretation that fortunately dominates within the more moderate Muslim nations and peoples, leads them to believe that anything is permissible in their jihad against the infidel. The Islamic fanatic considers it to be an article of faith to force the world to submit to his version of the one true god. The very word Islam means submission.

The communists also sought world domination and total submission but there is a fundamental difference between the two political faiths and that is that the Islamic fanatic believes he will be rewarded in the afterlife, whereas the communist is an atheist. In a practical sense, the communist movement was largely European and western in its origins and as such still retained vestiges of a western and Christian outlook, an outlook that placed paramount value to every human life.

One of the many myths regarding the Islamic terrorist movement is that there are fundamental differences between the Islam espoused by Osama bin Laden and the Taliban and opposed to that of the secular Baath Socialist Saddam Hussein. Like most American commentators, Barney Frank was unwittingly one of those who believed this myth when he stated in an interview before the Iraq war that he considered himself to be more Islamic than Saddam Hussein.

In fact, the Baath movement is not anti Islamic but is rather a merge between Islam and modern scientific Socialism. This was the intent of one of the primary founders of the Baath movement, educator Michel Aflaq, and this is reflected in Baath literature and on the official Baath website. While Saddam Hussein and bin Laden did not necessarily get along, they nevertheless both embraced the same radical Islamist worldview and would occasionally cooperate toward accomplishing those ends. America was viewed by both as the Great Satan because America stood, and still stands, as the greatest obstacle standing in the way toward their achieving their evil design.

I supported the war in Afghanistan and Iraq because I believed that both wars were consistent with the post 9/11 Bush Doctrine. That doctrine, articulated by President George W. Bush in his address to the nation following 9/11, was that the United States would retain the right to peruse terrorists who posed as a potential threat to the peace and stability of this country and that this policy would extend to any nation who harbored them. This doctrine rested on a solid foundation of international law and custom, which holds as one of its most historic and cherished principles, that a sovereign nation has a natural and inherent right to defend its people and property from any definable external threat.

The Iraq war, as I pointed out during my debates with the congressman, represented the very best American tradition of fighting for the sovereign rights of peoples oppressed either by repressive occupiers or dictatorships. This tradition goes back to our own revolution against the British tyrant King George III. The idea was articulated in 1823 by Secretary of State John Quincy Adams, the author of the Monroe Doctrine, which established the principle of sovereign rights in the western hemisphere. And this was the underlining policy behind our involvement in the Spanish-American War, the two World Wars, Korea, and Vietnam. Our nation was not seeking, in any of those cases, conquest or plunder.

Sometimes it is necessary for a nation to go to war in order to avoid a bigger and more destructive war. This lesson was learned the hard way by the liberal British Chancellor Neville Chamberlain after the failure of his mission to make peace with Hitler.

My opponent, despite protestations to the contrary during our debates, only reluctantly voted in favor of the war in Afghanistan. A politically active lawyer and resident of Brookline told me privately that he called the Congressman's office a few days after 9/11 to ask him about his position on the war against terrorism and where he stood on the invasion of Afghanistan. The Congressman confidently predicted that the nation would not go to war against the Taliban. Only one member of Congress, from Berkeley, California, ended up voting against the resolution to topple the Taliban regime.

My opponent voted against the Gulf War in 1991, a war that liberated Kuwait from Saddam Hussein's naked aggression, and he voted against the Iraq war of 2003. He subscribed to the unfounded conspiracy theory that President Bush lied to the American people regarding the existence of weapons of mass destruction in Iraq, claiming that the President knew in advance that Saddam had no such weapons but wanted to enter the war in order to promote a "geo-political agenda." Such an accusation against a sitting President, at a time of war, when America's prestige is on the line and the lives of American men and women in uniform are at risk, is a very serious one to make. The Congressman failed to provide any proof to back up this accusation after I asked him to do so during one of our debates.

Barney Frank has a consistent 24-year record of voting against defense appropriations and weapons programs. He voted against President Ronald Reagan's Strategic Defense Initiative known as Star Wars, which committed funds to research the feasibility of a program that would've rendered nuclear weapons obsolete. He voted to cut funding for missile programs such as the ICBM, MX, to cut funding for the B2 bomber, and to completely eliminate the Midgetman missile program in spite of the best advise of military experts. He voted to cut the CIA in the 1990's, at a time when CIA Director George Tenet, according to the 9/11 Commission Report, had told President Bill Clinton that the CIA was effectively in a state of war with international Islamic terrorists. Franks proposed cuts in the CIA budget came after the first World Trade Center attack and the attack on the Khobar Towers, which housed American military personnel in Saudi Arabia.

Barney Frank is a dove and a peacenik. He seems to subscribe to the utopian view that a weaker American military will cause the rest of the world to like us more. During our debates, Frank made vague references to the need for an international effort in Iraq as he alleged that President Bush had prevented this from occurring. It is my contention that a strong military, serving a government that places American interests first, is the right formula for America to not only garner more respect in the world, but more importantly, to secure the home front.

Social Security

In this election year, and true to form, the Democrats employed the usual scare tactic regarding Social Security with the claim that the Republicans would try to reduce the benefits. Never mind the fact that the Clinton Administration had in the 1990's floated the idea of rising the retirement age and means testing those who would receive benefits. In 1993, the Democratic dominated Congress, at the suggestion of the Clinton Administration, voted to tax Social Security. President Bush rescinded the Democrat Social Security tax.

During the campaign, my opponent criticized Federal Reserve Chairman Alan Greenspan for stating that Social Security benefits would most likely have to be reduced to accommodate the impending crunch that will accompany the retirement of the baby boomers. Yet, my opponent voted in favor of the Clinton tax on Social Security in 1993. Everyone in Congress, on both sides of the aisle, knows that Social Security is headed for an impending crisis. Most Democrats choose to ignore this issue and instead try to turn the tables by engaging in the worst kind of fear mongering and demagoguery against the Republicans. My opponent is at least honest enough to openly and, I might add, proudly, call for more taxes to deal with the crisis.

Frank says that President Bush's tax cuts are responsible for the impending crisis. Following this line of reasoning, the Congress would never be able to approve any tax cut. It has been acknowledged by credible economists that the Bush tax cuts stimulated the economy and helped turn the corner on a recession Bush inherited. The basic economic axiom at work here, and cited by President John F. Kennedy to justify his tax cuts in 1962, is that more capital left in the private sector leads to more investment, more consumer activity and exchanges, and ultimately to new jobs which means more taxable incomes. The practical result of tax cuts has proven to be that the government actually increases its revenue collection since there are more incomes to tax.

President Franklin D. Roosevelt signed the Social Security Act into law in 1938. The purpose of the program was to provide a pension for working people and their spouses upon retirement or death. The money, extracted out of the workingman's paycheck, was supposed to go into a secured Social Security Trust Fund. In 1965, President Lyndon B. Johnson wanted to simultaneously pay for escalating the Vietnam War and for the Great Society programs which constituted the largest expansion of the federal government since FDR's 1933 New Deal expansion to deal with the Great Depression.

Rather than resorting to the politically unpopular move of raising taxes, a move that would have led to an intense national debate on his policies, Johnson instead came up with the idea of raiding the Social Security Trust Fund. The money was replaced with slips of paper, IOU's, which have constituted a mortgage on the taxpayer ever since. There is presently no de facto Social Security Trust Fund. The contributions extracted out of the paychecks of working people are directly deposited into the U.S. Treasury as payments on these notes.

In one respect, Frank is right. Unless something is done, and if the system continues as it is, there will have to be massive tax increases to pay for the benefits of the Baby Boomers that will be reaching retirement age in the next several decades. Like most issues, Frank supports and even celebrates the regressive and economically constricting policy of tax increases on a population that is already paying over 40% of its hard earned income in taxes. Is there another way to deal with the problem?

Raising taxes to pay for Social Security is immoral. This is the equivalent of taking two dollars out of every one hundred dollars a working person earns to go to Social Security and then taking an additional two dollars out of the same one hundred dollars in order to ensure that the working person gets a portion of the original two dollars back. Besides being unfair, many working people, especially single people who die before retirement, never get any of their money back. The money disappears into the U.S. Treasury as payment for past government largess and waste.

Additionally, Barney Frank has consistently filed bills over his long career to extend Social Security benefits to people who never paid into the system. This has turned the system into a back door to welfare and is a major reason why Social Security has ballooned into the largest single expenditure the taxpayers are asked to absorb. And then, to add insult to injury, he wants working people to pay more taxes in order to receive anything back in the form of a benefit. This is blackmail. Roosevelt set up a system that would offer an annuity to those who paid into the system and that is what Social Security ought to be.

I don't claim to have a simple answer to the impending problem. No one in Congress can make such a claim. But I did make a suggestion during my debate in New Bedford, a suggestion that the Congressman mocked, that the government start by selling off most of the trillions of dollars in properties and assets it presently holds for no discernable reason. Vice President Al Gore was correct when he suggested the setting up of a "lock box" for Social Security, which is to say a separate fund that cannot be used for any purpose other than to pay benefits. The revenues resulting from the sale of government assets, which could include over half of the land surface of the country west of the Mississippi, could be placed in Al Gore's lock box.

A fundamental reform in the federal bureaucracy is in order. Besides possibly potentially unleashing hundreds of billions of dollars, government would function more efficiently and would therefore more ably serve our needs better. Funds unleashed as a result of this much-needed reform could also go into Al Gore's lock box. New retirees could then be offered a choice between receiving conventional social security benefits and receiving a flat figure buyout. This is what local municipalities and States sometimes do to reduce retirement costs.

I support President Bush in his proposal for a small percentage of the Social Security contribution to go into an interest bearing private investment account. As an employee of the federal government, my wife presently has the option of choosing where her retirement contribution goes. She can choose between five mutual funds, some higher risk, some lower risk. These funds are invested into both government instruments and private sector investments. The government maintains strict oversight regarding where the money is invested. Such a program could be established in the states to oversee the private investment of Social Security.

World Net Daily columnist and original thinker Sam Blumenfeld came up with an interesting and novel plan for retirement that would completely change the way we do Social Security altogether. He suggested in a column that the U.S. government put $1,000 into an interest bearing account for every child born or naturalized in the U.S. Thus, the child begins to earn interest from the day of birth or entry instead of waiting until he or she has a job. When that account reaches a certain point, the individual can then pay the government back the $1,000. By age 65, that interest bearing account could have accumulated as much as $500,000 or more for retirement. By then the retiree should be able to live on the interest alone. When the individual dies, the remaining money can be passed on to his or her heirs.

As it stands now, the government extracts the money out of the paycheck of the workingman and the money goes directly into the U. S. Treasury where it earns no interest. The government decides when the worker retires. The money disappears back into the U.S. Treasury upon the death of the worker and his or her spouse. Social Security has been turned into nothing more than a form of taxation.

A private fund would earn the wage earner interest on the hard earned investment. This money would accumulate over the years to the point where the worker could raise a substantial nest egg upon retirement. When the retiree dies, the nest egg he worked his entire life to build would then be passed on to his heirs. What a great way to increase private ownership and to reduce poverty in this country.

Streamlining the Government

Why can't the government consolidate and streamline the massive web of agencies that have been built up over generations? Many of these agencies are redundant, not serving in the public interest, or have outlived their usefulness. Such reforms should not be viewed as a liberal versus a conservative issue but simply as a good government policy. All Americans should insist on a streamlined and efficient government operating at the lowest possible cost to the taxpayer. The reason the liberal establishment has embraced the idea of big bureaucratic government is because much of the money and power that emanates from such a system accrues to them and their dependent constituencies.

Big and cumbersome government is good for special interests where liberals dominate. Big government also tends to intrude into the lives of the rest of us, which is another big benefit for the liberal elitist who sees himself as possessing a superior intelligence and a right to meddle into the affairs of those of us who don't enjoy the benefit of being as enlightened.

Social Security, funded out of the hard-earned paycheck of every workingman and woman, can be saved. I believe that the social safety net, funding for transportation projects, and other services can continue without raising taxes. The answer is not more taxes but rather reducing the size and cost of government. Congress creates bureaucracies and Congress can undo bureaucracies. Congress, which is the branch of government that holds the purse strings and has the power to tax, ought to represent the taxpayer and, as such, ought to make sure that the taxpayer dollar is well spent and, when possible, saved. Too many Congressmen have forgotten the taxpayers and instead have come to represent special interests and the power of the government itself.

Why can't the agencies and bureaucracies of government be consolidated and, if possible, eliminated? An historic example of such elimination would be that of the Interstate Commerce Commission (ICC), the first federal regulatory agency in U.S. history. Created in 1887, as a response to abusive railroad practices, the agency primarily functioned as a regulator of railroads, and later as a regulator of trucking companies, interstate bus lines, and infrastructure. By 1966, most of the functions of the ICC had been absorbed by other agencies or eliminated. What was left was transferred to the newly-established Department of Transportation. Yet the ICC continued to cruise along for another 29 years until it was finally abolished in 1995, saving the taxpayer countless millions. How many more ICC's are out there rambling along in the twilight unnoticed? Based on his record, we won't be able to depend on Barney Frank to investigate.

One of the reasons the Department of Homeland Security was created was to address the problem of the multiple agencies and committees charged with dealing with various aspects of national security. In fact, one of the reasons why our government was caught so unprepared on 9/11 was because of the existence of these literally hundreds of agencies dealing with security related issues. This led to a state of paralysis. The recommendations of the 9/11 Commission Report call for a consolidation of these agencies into approximately a dozen groupings, under the auspices of the Department of Homeland Security. Why can't this be done in every agency in government?

There are several practical steps Congress can take toward streamlining the government and balancing the budget. Following are a few suggestions:

1. Impose an immediate one-year moratorium on all non National Security related spending and hiring. This freeze would be followed by any annual increase to be pegged to the rate of inflation.

2. Insist on a pay as you go policy. Government would be only allowed to spend out of already received revenues.

3. Audit every government agency and financial grant over a certain amount with an eye toward eliminating waste and fraud and consolidation.

4. Passage of a balanced budget bill that forces the government to balance the Federal budget every year except in times of declared war or national emergency.

5. Passage of a line item veto for the President so as to remove pork barrel add ons to bills before Congress.

6. Strengthening of whistleblower laws and the establishment of a permanent nonpartisan congressional committee empowered to hear private testimony from whistleblowers.

7. The establishment of a discretionary fund to help pay for natural disasters and other crisis so as to lessen the impact on the budget.

8. Strengthening of lobbyist laws so that government officials entering the private sector would have to wait five years before becoming a lobbyist.

Health Care

During our debates, the Congressman came out in favor of universal health care, which is to say he supports socialized, government-managed health care. This was a popular stand for the Democratic Presidential candidates during the primaries. Senator Joe Lieberman made the most conservative and least expensive proposal of the Democrats. His plan would've cost the taxpayer an estimated $60 billion annually which, if implemented, would've likely ended up costing $100 billion annually. Such expenditures would've driven up the tax rate on working people to over 50%. No wonder Barney Frank is a supporter.

Like all socialist schemes, socialized medicine has already proven to be a complete failure. Canada saves money by rationing health care and refusing to cover certain things such as painkillers for women undergoing a difficult childbirth. Waiting lists are long and resources are scarce. France has a socialized government health system, which, at its dysfunctional worst, let 30,000 elderly people die because of the heat. Clearly the American system is the best in the world because it still retains vestiges of the free market, while ensuring access to consumers.

What then is to be done about the rising cost of healthcare and healthcare for the uninsured? Steps can be taken which will lead to a lowering of the cost. Senator John Kerry, the Democratic Presidential nominee, proposed, for example, that Medicare purchase drugs and health services from the lowest bidder. This huge agency should be using its considerable leveraging power to negotiate the best possible price for drugs.

Presently, drug companies and health care providers spend tens of millions on lobbyists, many of whom are former Congressmen and congressional staffers, who try to get Medicare to buy at the highest price. This has driven up the cost so high that individuals and municipalities are now turning to socialist Canada to buy American drugs. Even the Canadians are buying the drugs at a cheaper price than our own Medicare system. The Democrats are not in a position to criticize since this has been going on for decades, and yet they cynically decided to run with this issue in an election year.

As for the shortage of flu vaccine, an issue that came up both in the Presidential debates and in my debates with the Congressman, one of the reasons why we are so dependent on the British and Swedish is because American companies were so susceptible to law suits that they closed their businesses. While malpractice penalties are necessary, the compensatory damage awards have gotten so far out of proportion that they have driven up the cost of health care and insurance, a cost passed on to the consumer. These huge damage settlements put companies at competitive risk and have caused doctors and health care providers to restrict their activities for fear of being sued. That's why we need tort reform, so that people like Senator John Edwards, the Democratic Vice Presidential nominee, cannot make a fortune while putting legitimate drug manufacturers and health care providers out of business. Democrats oppose tort reform because they derive a large percentage of their contributions from trial lawyers.

I support the President's discount prescription cards for seniors who are having trouble paying for their drugs. Regarding those who are uninsured, Massachusetts has a program in which the major insurance companies pay into a fund that covers catastrophic cases and those who are indigent. Hospitals and medical centers in Massachusetts receive subsidies for accepting the indigent and the uninsured. I support a reasonable expansion of these programs with federal involvement. In 2004, my opponent voted against a bill before Congress that would've made it easier for small businesses to form purchasing chains for the purpose of purchasing health insurance for their employees at lower bulk rates. Congress ought to by helping the private sector with such plans.

I also support the President's proposal for private medical savings accounts. These funds would be paid by an employer as a benefit and also taken out of the paycheck or the wage earner and deposited into an interest bearing private account. A portion of the account could then go toward the purchase of a catastrophic health insurance policy. The rest of the accumulating funds could be used to pay for routine health care in the form of a health debit card. This program, with the funds transferable between jobs, would lessen the dependence on company-provided health plans and lead to more choice and control over health care by the individual. This is all a part of what President Bush meant when he talked about an ownership society.

Abortion

Over 30 years after the Roe vs. Wade Supreme Court decision legalizing abortion, this issue remains one of the greatest and thorniest moral questions of our times. While I support a women's right to choose to abort her unborn baby, I also contend, for both religious and scientific reasons, that abortion is immoral and should not be done except if there are sound medical reasons that would warrant such an extreme measure. The killing of the unborn child is something that has coarsened our society, cheapened human life, and has contributed to a culture of death.

Women must retain, however, the right to do just that with their unborn child at least in the early stages of a pregnancy. As much as I despise the barbaric practice, the government cannot force a woman to carry a pregnancy. To do so would be both coercive and impractical. If abortion were to be legally banned, women who wanted one would have to be put in prison until the baby was born. Women who had abortions would have to be tried for murder, sent to prison, and possibly executed.

I was proud to be endorsed by the Massachusetts Citizens for Life. While my position on abortion is not consistent with theirs, they endorsed my candidacy partially because my opponent is radically pro abortion. The congressman voted against banning the heinous practice of partial birth abortion, and against an act that called for penalties for physical violence against an unborn child. I support both measures. Frank has a 100% rating with the pro abortion groups Planned Parenthood and NARAL.

While I am pro choice, I am also opposed to any government funding of abortion, domestically or internationally. Given the fact that such a large percentage of Americans oppose abortion on moral and practical grounds, it is not appropriate for taxpayer monies to underwrite abortion.

The more practical way to reduce the number of abortions in this country is through education, as opposed to an outright ban. While attending the annual Massachusetts Citizens for Life banquet as a guest of the eminent physician and former Republican Senatorial candidate Dr. Mildred Jefferson, who has been on the forefront of the anti abortion movement, I viewed a graphic film that showed exactly what abortion is. I would hope that the "pro-choice" community would join me in insisting that the public at large view this film. If we tell the truth about abortion, we will be on the road toward ensuring that abortion is truly, in the words of former President Bill Clinton, "legal, safe, and rare."

Moral Values

There are two threads that run through the Torah, which, as a traditional Jew, I believe is the repository of the divine word of the creator. Those two threads are contained in the laws of Moses, revealed to the Israelites at Sinai. On the one hand, there are strict commandments in the Torah regarding what is proper in terms of personal and professional relationships between individuals and between nations. On the other hand there is the maxim "love your neighbor as yourself." The Israelites were commanded at Sinai to obey the laws of Moses while at the same time to tolerate each other.

Our nation was founded on these same two seemingly contradictory maxims. On the one hand, our system of laws and our sense of ethics and morality are derived from the judeo-Christian code of Sinai. On the other hand, we believe in the old saying, "government that governs best governs least." Our success as a society has largely derived from our ability to balance these two ideas.

The art and science of governance in America, particularly legislative governance, whether the legislative body is a local school board, board of alderman, city council, state legislature, or the U.S. Congress, is the ongoing process of balancing these two ideas. On the one hand, the government must not enact laws that directly contradict the moral code upon which our system of laws are based, lest we become dis-moored from our moral underpinnings. On the other hand, government must step aside and allow for the maximum of individual freedom and choice. Legislatures must constantly weigh and measure both of these factors when crafting legislation as social mores change at various times in either direction.

I believe that at present, our society and our nation has become too weighted in the direction of maximum freedom and is straying too far away from the moral code. For example, the government can play a role in helping families to protect the innocence of children by prosecuting child pornography and obscenity cases. The government should investigate and crack down on the multi billion-dollar pornography industry. Local and state governments ought to set dress codes in school and education ought to be based on a morality-based curriculum as opposed to one based on situational ethics and moral relativism.

"Frank's opponent plays the gay card"

I shouldn't have been surprised to read the New Bedford Standard-Times headline "Frank's opponent plays the gay card (3/14)." A few days before the sensational banner headline at the top of the Sunday "Perspectives" section, the reporter called on my cell phone to accuse me of authorizing a fundraising email letter targeting "fundamentalist Christians." My sarcastic response was that I had authorized an email targeting known conservative donors, many of whom might very well be…gasp…gasp…Christians.

The evidence offered in the article that I had played the "gay card" was that the fundraising email letter in question included the following statement: "Having served 12 terms in Congress, he (Frank) has become perhaps the most well-known and notorious gay rights activist in America…Barney Frank is the most outspoken proponent of gay marriage in America."

This was a reference to important public policy issues, specifically gay marriage, hate crimes legislation, and ENDA, a bill granting special protection to gay men and women regarding employment. My opponent and I hold opposing views on these issues. These are legitimate differences that call for a substantive debate. The email also mentioned my opponent's Congressional reprimand for activities that revolved around his relationship with a male prostitute. Again, this was a matter of public record. The Boston Globe had called for the Congressman's resignation at the time. To not mention an issue that is mentioned occasionally by the media and by the Congressman himself would've been the equivalent of letting an important portion of my opponent's record, one that illustrates a pattern of irresponsibility, slip down the Orwellian memory hole.

In order to shift the attention away from these and other issues, the Standard-Times article launched into a smear campaign against me as someone who had something against gay men and women. The false sub-title "Morse addresses

Congressman's sexuality in fund-raising e-mail" was justified by the dredging up of an old and obscure reference I had written in an article about aggressive homosexuals and homosexuals involved in Nazism. These references were not part of the fundraising email as implied in the article, but rather were sent in to the paper by the Congressman.

The Standard-Times article appeared on March 14, about two weeks after the Massachusetts Supreme Judicial Court ruling declaring gay marriage as legal. In the heated atmosphere immediately following that ruling, these references, which were psycho-social commentary too complex to delve into in the heat of a campaign, took on a different meaning than that which was intended, as both Frank and the paper knew they would.

Barney Frank and the Standard-Times knew full well that I had nothing against gay men and women. In order to marginalize my positions so as to avoid a reasonable public policy debate, they instead chose to conduct a witch-hunt to prove my guilt, to try me in the press, and to try to destroy my reputation. These references, isolated and taken out of context, were all they could come up with after months of close scrutiny. It's easy to frame a conservative as anti gay when he says things that liberals might say. I was hammered for this regularly during the campaign in classic agitprop style.

The Congressman has a record of attacking people that dare oppose what he considers to be the gay agenda. This created an intimidating atmosphere, which is why I relied on rote responses when asked my position, for example, on an issue like gay marriage. My response was: "Along with Presidential candidate John Kerry, former Vermont Governor Howard Dean, and former President Bill Clinton, I uphold the concept of marriage between a man and a woman."

A demonstration of the volatile atmosphere in which I was operating occurred when a Boston Globe reporter interviewed me in relation to a story he was writing on Frank's no vote on the Amber Alert bill early in the campaign. The Amber Alert system is set up to help law enforcement apprehend child kidnappers.

The entire all Democratic Massachusetts congressional delegation, except Barney Frank, and all but 25 congressmen nationally, as well as a unanimous Senate, voted in favor of the non-partisan Amber Alert bill. Since the bill became law in June 2003, over 150 children have been rescued from kidnappers. Astonishingly, the Congressman had responded to the Globe inquiry regarding his no vote by stating that he had voted no on Amber Alert because he was opposed to two "Republican add-ons" to the bill. He stated that the two add ons he objected to were a law calling for a mandatory minimum prison sentence for a second-time convicted child molester and the Rave Act, which specifically helped federal prosecutors go after clubs which promote use of the drug "Ecstasy."

The Globe reporter asked me if I thought Frank's no vote on Amber Alert was in any way connected to his sexual orientation. My sincere response was that I had absolutely no doubt in my mind that gay men and women would join with me in supporting the Amber Alert system. I suggested like everyone else, gay men and women have children and young siblings, relatives and friends and that they wanted to see them protected, which is why I knew they would join with me in disgust over the Congressman's no vote.

Shortly after the Globe article was published, I was invited over to the office of the liberal Boston Phoenix where, among other things, a reporter browbeat me on gay issues. Since I didn't answer his questions in the manner that he had hoped, and since the Phoenix felt they had nothing to go on in what appeared to be an attempt to paint me as a some sort of a raving buck-toothed homophobe and as a right-wing Neanderthal, the paper chose instead to remain silent altogether regarding the 4th district race. I guess the guiding maxim at the Boston Phoenix must be that if you can't find anything bad to write about a conservative, don't write anything at all.

I believe that most people consider a person's sexual orientation to be a private and personal matter and would just as soon leave it that way. Frank, on the other hand, plays the gay card himself by regularly injecting the issue into the public discourse. He uses the issue to cast himself as a victim. He injects the issue into the national discourse as he advocates for changes in law and public policy.

Frank calls for laws that favor gay men and women. Therefore, since the public and their elected representatives are being asked to accept such laws, the discussion ought to be enjoined in an atmosphere of thoughtfulness and care. The three issues the public is being asked to consider are gay marriage, hate crimes legislation and ENDA, the employment related bill.

Elected representatives ought to be able to debate these legitimate issues since changes in the law might have a profound impact on our society. The passage of such laws, for example, might involve an indirect transfer of wealth or further involvement of government into the private sector. As a candidate for Congress and as a citizen of this country, I insist upon a reasoned and dispassionate debate to be held in an atmosphere that is not rife with intimidation and fear. I also insist that any legislation that is crafted and enacted into law ought to be handled by the votes of officials elected to represent the people as opposed to by the fiat decree of appointed judges and bureaucrats. This is how things should be done in a democracy.

I will end this segment on a sad note. Barney Frank entered the U. S. Congress in 1981, the same year in which the AIDS epidemic became a crisis in this country and elsewhere in the world. At that time, AIDS was hitting the gay male population particularly hard. Two friends of mine, one a classmate from my childhood years in Quincy and the other a co-worker, contracted this dread disease. Both men were struck down in the prime of their young lives. Both men suffered and died horrible and unspeakable deaths.

In the 1980's, before the development of drugs that help AIDS patients stay healthy, AIDS was a sure death sentence. Barney Frank was one of the nation's most prominent defenders of gay rights in those years and would become one of the nations most visible gay leaders himself after publicly coming out in the mid 1980's. Yet Barney Frank, as far as I know, never once used his position of influence within the gay community or at large to come out publicly against promiscuous sex or to discourage sexual practices that were generally associated with the spread of AIDS.

The Congressman did not forcefully advocate for the most basic and common sense health measures to lessen the possible exposure of gay men to AIDS such as the shutting down of gay bath houses and other common sense measures. In fact, Frank was proud of his sponsorship of an amendment to the Immigration and Nationality Act that allowed people with AIDS to enter into this country with visas. I believe this is the first time in recorded history where a nation offered visas to people with a contagious and communicable disease. There is no way of knowing if or how many people were put at risk or may have contracted AIDS as a result of this incredibly misguided policy.

The Congressman could have used his position of influence to stop unspeakable suffering and death but instead he chose to do nothing. He could have treated AIDS for what it was, a disease, nothing more and nothing less, instead of as a political football. Tens of thousands of men might be alive today if Barney Frank had taken a leadership role in a community where his word was taken seriously.

"Why I'm a Right-Wing Extremist"

I was an Internet columnist and I expected when I entered the race that the columns would be critiqued by my opponent and by the media especially the one satirically entitled "Why I'm a Right-Wing Extremist."

Suffice it to say, the column in question proves that I had no political ambitions before deciding to run. For the sake of accuracy, the column should've been entitled "Why They Call Me a Right-Wing Extremist" but that's all water under the bridge.

The point of the column was that anyone, including a liberal, runs the risk of being denounced as a "right-wing extremist" if that person is not politically correct on an issue and dares to state the position publicly. At the time that I wrote that column, I was becoming more publicly identified with conservative ideas. I was stunned by the small minded and provincial reaction by many of my so-called enlightened friends, family members and colleagues.

The columns, and a full-length book I authored entitled "The Nazi Connection to Islamic Terrorism" which is a biography of the Grand Mufti of Jerusalem, deal primarily with a subject that is still too taboo for polite company. That subject is the history of communism and it's political and cultural influence on America. I hope to live long enough to see the day when our society progresses to the point where such a study will no longer be viewed as controversial, but rather for what it is, a simple attempt at examining the forces of history.

I was prepared to discuss the columns knowing full well that they contained some bombshells. I had, after all, taken on some very sacred cows both on the left and on the right. My lack of political experience, however, led me to assume that they would not be thrust into the forefront of the race. Was I wrong about that!

Predictably, the Congressman extracted things out of context, magnified them, isolated them, and then exaggerated and misrepresented their meaning. For the purpose of brevity and so as not to bore the reader I will confine myself to addressing one issue specifically brought up by the Congressman because it is the most egregious, the most oft repeated, and the most misrepresented.

The issue that took on the proportion of political legend during the campaign was the utterly false charge made by the Congressman that I had written that the Clinton Administration was somehow behind the bombing of the Murrah Federal Building in Oklahoma City.

I had personal reasons for writing about that terrorist attack. My wife Barbara worked as an attorney for the government in a federal building in Boston that was similar to the Murrah building. What kind of a person would I be if I permitted my wife, the mother of my child, to go to work there if I thought that the government might blow up its own building? As I said at the debate in New Bedford when this accusation was made by Frank, "This is an obnoxious lie."

I was a talk show host around the time of the attack. Like many in the media, I covered the story. I interviewed three people who I believed had credibility on this issue, retired Brigadier General Benton Parton, considered an expert on munitions, Oklahoma State Senator Charles Key, who had conducted extensive research, and reporter Jayna Davis, who has since authored a book linking the attack to Islamic terrorists. They made the case that the Oklahoma City attack involved something larger than two guys and a truck full of explosive fertilizer. My article was based on their conclusions. They did not suggest government complicity.

There was evidence that certain local government officials had some advance information that something violent might occur that day at the Murrah Building. No one, except for the terrorists themselves, knew the building was going to be bombed. A memorandum had gone out to federal employees nationally a few days before the attack warning them to be cautious and to watch for suspicious activity.

When the issue came up during one of the debates, I noted the parallels between events leading up to the Oklahoma City attack and those leading up to the attack on September 11th. The 9/11 Commission Report documented how various government officials had prior knowledge that something was going to happen on 9/11. I pointed out that the lesson of Oklahoma City as well as the lesson of 9/11 was that certain government agencies were too apathetic, too secretive, and too paralyzed by bureaucracy to respond. As a result, nothing was done in either case.

I also had made note of the fact that in the aftermath of both attacks, certain government officials wanted to downplay the investigation. In my opinion this was motivated by an attempt to cover up incompetence.

When I wrote the column, I was concerned that certain members of Congress were over reacting to the crisis and turning the situation into a political football. There were debates at the time regarding whether anti-domestic terrorism legislation should be passed to deal with the emergency. Eventually, an anti terrorism bill was passed which provided a foundation for the passage, years later, of the USA Patriot Act.

During the deliberations over this legislation, proposals were being made such as the authorizing of trials, which would deny the accused the right to face his accuser or to hear evidence. To my way of thinking, these ideas were more typical of a banana republic than of the greatest Republic in history.

Ironically, Barney Frank was a supporter of many of these measures back then. I interviewed him at the time on my radio program and I was astonished and troubled by his stated positions in favor of this ill-conceived legislation. At the same time, Frank voted against a bill that would give the government the right to use secret evidence to deport a non citizen accused of being a terrorist.

Since that time, the Congressman seems to have taken a 180-degree turn and is now fashioning himself as a defender of civil liberties. In his opposition to the USA Patriot Act, he has compared Attorney General John Ashcroft to the Communist Chinese dictator.

Gerald Posner, the author of "Why America Slept" describes Frank as a civil libertarian when explaining why he sponsored legislation that made it easier for potential terrorists to obtain visas and enter the country legally. It is an interesting contradiction. On the one hand, the Congressman wants to crack down on domestic terrorists, on the other hand he puts out a welcome mat for foreign terrorists. I'm not going to attempt to fathom the inner working's of the Congressman's mind on these issues, but I will venture that he repeatedly ignores the lessons of history.

One of the other issues the Congressman, and the media in general, have had with my articles is that I occasionally express a religious point of view. While I'm not personally overtly religious and while I'm not a moralist, I nevertheless contend that this country was established on biblically-based Judeo-Christian law and values and I hold those values in high esteem. My written references to this seem to drive some liberals nuts. Articles written about my candidacy occasionally included quotes taken from articles I wrote that make reference to God and to moral values. These quotes would be woven into the text in such a manner as would indicate that the reporter assumed the reader would be repulsed.

One hot button issue brought up both by the Congressman on Newsnight and by a reporter from the Patriot Ledger, was that I had made reference in a column to the theory of evolution by referring to it as just a theory and not proven science. I didn't realize that by doing this, I would be in essence stepping on the holy grail of the secular liberal establishment. When Frank brought it up on Newsnight, he looked like he was about to have a meltdown.

My articles were certainly controversial. They reflected a sensibility born out of the new media. My political involvement began when I became a radio talk show host in 1996. Since then, I've been a syndicated website columnist, a self published author, and a host of a local cable TV talk show. All of these are forms of the new and emerging media.

The new media operates in an environment that is less censored, more open to diverse opinion, and more freewheeling. It is the new frontier of thought and expression. The emerging technologies of today, which permit instant and unfiltered communication through the Internet, inexpensive self-publishing, cable access, and of course radio, are quickly changing the way we communicate and I am on the forefront of that trend. I very well may be the first new media figure to wade into politics in a major way and to take on an establishment figure such as Barney Frank.

My intention here is to in no way denigrate the important and enduring influence of the mainstream media. We need the establishment media to homogenize things and to help maintain a semblance of unity in thought and culture. Mainstream views must maintain their rightful place. The new media is simply an alternative that lends balance, provides an outlet for expression to the everyman, and constitutes an incubator of ideas. The two forms of media both compete with and complement each other, borrow from each other, and offer a system of checks and balances in the marketplace of public opinion.

The Case against Frank

The immigration legislation sponsored by Barney Frank which made it easier for terrorists to enter the country legally is an example of what happens when laws are passed that, however well intended, are not based on reality. There are consequences that emanate from misguided initiatives and those consequences can involve terrible failure and immense tragedy. Barney Frank stated his political philosophy toward the end of the campaign when he told the Brookline Tab, in response to why he was running for re-election, that he had "not yet finished his work…Why? Because the world's not perfect yet. And that's my mission—to make it less imperfect."

This statement reveals an underlying belief on the part of the Congressman, one that many liberals embrace to varying degrees, and that belief holds that government ought to be used to change human nature, to ultimately bring about human perfection. Subscribers to this view see government as an instrument of change and the "progressive" government official is viewed as a "change-agent."

Too often, those who have embraced such a philosophy historically, those who have seen themselves as more enlightened than the rest of us, when not constrained by a constitution or by a population that sufficiently understands inherent rights, eventually form a clique of dictators as happened in Nazi Germany, Communist Russia, and today in parts of the Middle East. The simple truth is that in America, Frank and his soul mates, those who are inclined to worship the power of government and who view those of us who reject their views as anti-government, will never get too far. I'm not implying that Frank and his "progressive" cohorts are seeking to become dictators; they respect the Constitution and the rule of law as much as the rest of us. Nevertheless, I contend that dictatorship would be the ultimate manifestation of their philosophy, however well intentioned, if it were to ever become enthroned.

Frank is a hyper-nationalist who supports national health care; national education, national welfare, and national police power in the form of hate crimes legislation. I support the opposite, which is individual rights, free market solutions, and limited government. To Frank's way of thinking, this makes me "right-wing." Nothing could be further from the truth unless it is acknowledge that the Nazi movement, like its totalitarian cousin the Communist movement, was left wing.

Such political faiths brook no in-betweens, which is why Frank accused me, and conservatives in general during our debates, of being anti-government. During our joint appearance on the TV show Greater Boston with Emily Rooney, Frank made a reference to "right-wing" politicians who don't agree with him on the need to raise taxes as being inherently anti government.

At its very core, this is an expression of the philosophy of the totalitarian. Fortunately for the rest of us, Frank's hyper nationalist approach to government is kept in check by the chains of the Constitution of the United States of America. America is not on a mission to make the world less imperfect but rather to recognize that it is the inherent right of the individual to mold his own life and destiny. Our judeo-Christian ethos impart to us that man is by nature imperfect and that only the creator is perfect. Therefore, government serves as a vehicle to protect us from ourselves in our imperfectability. The American approach has been that government both protects freedom and stays out of the way so that freedom can flourish and prosperity can ensue.

The 4th congressional district is essentially made up of three parts. The northern more liberal part includes my hometown of Brookline, Newton, and, increasingly, Wellesley. These communities are largely made up of people who are in the higher levels of the economic scale. A high number of the residents of these communities commute to Boston or along the high-tech belt that corresponds with Route #128 and forms a ring around Boston. The central part of the district is more conservative and more middle and working class suburban.

It's easier for citizens in the relatively affluent communities of the northern part of the district to support liberal policies that include high taxes and big and intrusive government because taking such a stand makes them feel less guilty about their relatively prosperous lifestyle. High taxes and big and intrusive government are not likely to affect them since large numbers of them enjoy a higher degree of job and economic security. The liberal feels that government should do the job of caring for the less fortunate so that they don't have to think about it too much. They can afford to be liberal but they have no idea how much their big government advocacy, however well intended, actually hurts working people and the poor.

The southern part of the district centers on the great old whaling and manufacturing port of New Bedford, which is where I originally announced my candidacy at the Shawmut Diner. That center of talk and good food is owned by my friend and fellow conservative radio talk show host Phil Paleologos. I set up my headquarters in the Cherry Building, a few blocks from City Hall, which is managed by Rob Sudduph, a true entrepreneur who transformed the building during the year I was there from an empty shell into a bustling center of activity. Besides all the new shops and offices, the building now hosts a new annex to the University of Massachusetts—Dartmouth. New Bedford is the true heart and soul of the district and a city that I came to love.

While the people in New Bedford and the surrounding communities are largely independent minded, there are still too many who are fooled by the old and failed liberal rhetoric of Barney Frank. He drones on about increasing taxes on those who make over $200,000 per year and on Bill Gates. That old class consciousness style of rhetoric plays to the lowest common denominator in all of us which is jealousy of our more successful neighbor and a sense of entitlement with regard to getting a piece of that success. Never mind the fact that that the middle class, the small businessman, and the lower middle class taxpayer will end up paying for those tax increases. Never mind mentioning the fact that these tax increases hurt business and job creation, shrink the economy, and contribute to the growth of wasteful and freedom constricting government bureaucracy.

It became clear to me early on in the campaign that New Bedford suffers from a corrupt and stagnant political culture. After over a half century of control by the Democratic Party, the political atmosphere in the city has become downright putrid. Barney Frank can get away with a dismal voting record in Congress with regard to business interests and even reside over a bank merger during the campaign that resulted in the layoff of over 350 people in downtown New Bedford while holding his position as the ranking Democrat on the House Banking and Finance Committee because he is a part of that calcified and corroded system. Frank has done little to secure significant grants for the region other than for his artsy-fartsy friends who maintain historic buildings in the downtown area that are beautiful to look at but that seem to have very little if anything going on inside. Frank has done nothing noticeable in his long tenure regarding the securing of funding for the much needed New Bedford-Fall River commuter rail other than passing the buck.

Many newspapers in the district endorsed Barney Frank for Congress in the last days of the campaign. These same papers generally demonstrated grace and class by also congratulating me for my hard work and effort even if they didn't agree with my politics. The Taunton Gazette actually did a piece that came close to endorsing me. In the Standard Times endorsement of Barney Frank the paper didn't even have the decency to mention my name. Instead they slipped in the infamous and untactful smear at the end of their endorsement. "critics of Frank expressed a hope that the gay marriage decision in Massachusetts might fuel an anti-gay backlash that would help Frank's opponent. But over the years, the people of this congressional district have shown in election after election that Rep. Frank's sexuality is not a factor in judging his fitness for office."

When I started gathering signatures to get my name placed on the ballot, I noticed that Barney Frank had what can only be described as a cult following. Certain people refused to sign my nomination papers because they didn't want Frank to have an opponent. Their hostility was based on what appeared to me to be an almost blind and slavish loyalty to the Congressman, sort of like hero worship. Most people I approached were perfectly civil toward me and many said that they thought they liked Barney Frank and while they weren't exactly sure why, they would probably vote for him. Others promised to support me only if I agreed that I could not win. Others agreed that it was time to return a semblance of balance and reason to the Commonwealth.

Conclusion

On the Saturday before the election, WRKO radio talk show hosts Pat Whitley and Marjorie Claparood interviewed both Congressman Frank and me. Toward the end of the segment with Frank, both hosts waxed nostalgic regarding how much they personally liked the congressman. The warm and fuzzy segment was concluded with Claporood's gushing that everybody loves you Barney, you're the most popular congressman in the state.

This is an illustration of a principle that became clear to me early on in the race. Personality and perception will usually trump the truth when it comes to electing a leader. Niccolo Machiavelli wrote about this in his famous political tome "the Prince" when he pointed out that a leader must create an illusion in order to lead and that the illusion need not be constrained by truths. What often counts most in an election is how things seem rather than how they are.

My opponent has woven an effective illusion and he's got a personality to pull it off. I don't discount the importance of personality; a leader needs to fall back on personal skills, especially in the event that he must convince people to accept an unpopular decision.

The truth, however, is important and the illusion has consequences. This is why my opponent, when confronted with my truth telling, had to claim that I was being untruthful. Pay no attention to the man behind the curtain my opponent wants you to hear, I am the great and powerful Oz and I have spoken. My truthfulness, as a candidate for Congress and previously as a talk show host and as a writer, would prove to be both my greatest strength and my greatest weakness.

I received 25% of the vote. John Kerry, the favorite son, drew out record numbers of Democrats who voted the straight party ticket. About 12% of the voters in the district are Republican. All of the Republican challengers for Congress in Massachusetts and all candidates running for State Senate and State Representative, except for State Senator Scott Brown, lost their bids for election.

The Kerry victory in Massachusetts owed a great deal to emotional factors. The Boston Red Sox had won the World Series after an 82-year losing streak just a few weeks before Election Day. The New England Patriots had won the Super Bowl Championship. A victory for John Kerry's would've been the equivalent of a triple trifecta. Besides Rhode Island, Massachusetts was the only state in which Kerry carried every county. Never mind that Kerry represented regressive ideas and policies that hurt working people and national security. Many Massachusetts voters wanted to continue the winning streak. I believe, however, that this State will vote more conservatively the next time around. The State doesn't exist in a vacuum.

Massachusetts is the cradle of liberty, the birthplace of American democracy. Leaders of the caliber of John Adams, Abigail Adams, Samuel Adams, James Otis, and John Hancock once risked their necks to promote individual rights and liberty against the ever-increasing authoritarianism of the big and intrusive government of King George III. Massachusetts led the way back then and Massachusetts can lead again today.

Our state has made progress as evidenced by the election of Mitt Romney but our Congressional delegation remains mired in the old and discredited ways of the past. The Massachusetts liberal Democratic cookie-cutter delegation continues along on the path of big and intrusive government, appeasement abroad, and rule by judicial decree.

As I had predicted, President George W. Bush won a significant victory over John Kerry and both houses of the U.S. Congress picked up Republican seats. We can at least expect a reasonably conservative and therefore a genuinely progressive government for the next couple of years. Virtually every candidate for federal office nationally, including most Democrats, except for my opponent, ran on a conservative platform of fiscal reform and low taxes.

John Kerry is back in the Senate where he will likely remain until his term expires in four years. President Bush will remain in office for four more years and both houses of Congress will likely remain in Republican hands for the rest of the decade and well into the next. Barney Frank, a liberal minority within a minority party, will continue as a Congressman out of the mainstream with nowhere to turn. I will be doing my part to change the political culture of the district and the state. Change doesn't happen overnight, it takes hard work. I intend to stick with it.

As this book goes to press, the news has just come in that Barney Frank has been unceremoniously dumped from the Congressional Committee on Home-land Security. I had called for his resignation due to his sponsorship of the Frank Amendment legislation, which made it easier for terrorists to enter the country legally. I had faxed a press release to that effect to virtually every Republican in Congress including Rep. Christopher Cox, the chairman of the committee. I had discussed the issue at length during the campaign, including on several popular TV shows in Boston and the issue had been reported on in the Boston Globe. Frank responded to my charge with the incredibly lame claim that Tom Keane, the chairman of the 9/11 Commission, had absolved him of guilt in a private conversation. I suspect that Barney Frank was sacked because he had become a liability and an embarrassment.

About the Author

Host of the radio talk show *Morse Code*, Chuck Morse is the owner of City Metro Enterprises, a national advertising distribution company. *Talkers Magazine* rated Mr. Morse one of the hot upcoming talk show hosts of 2002. Mr. Morse ran for Congress in the 4th congressional district of Massachusetts in 2004 and lives in Brookline with his wife Barbara and 5-year-old daughter.

Index

0-595-33855-0

www.ingramcontent.com/pod-product-compliance
Lightning Source LLC
Chambersburg PA
CBHW021251280526
45784CB00005B/2325

9780595338559